Bix
10.—

From one China to the other

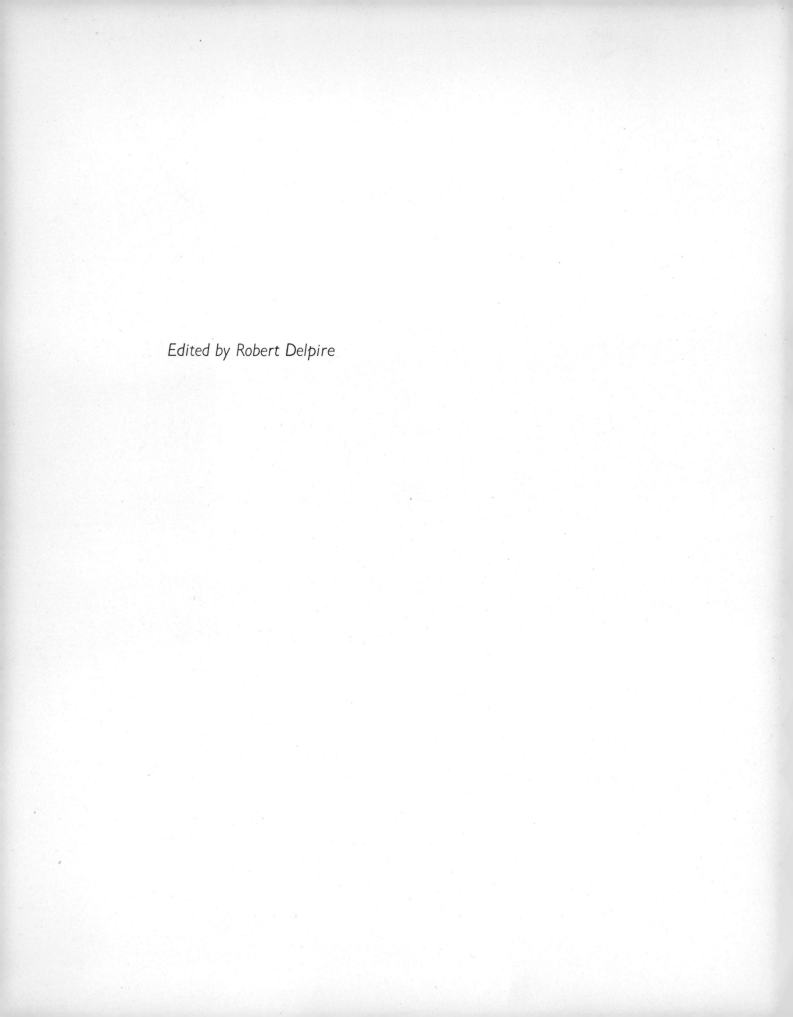

Edited by Robert Delpire

FROM ONE CHINA
TO THE OTHER

Photographs by Henri Cartier-Bresson
Text by Han Suyin, pseud.

Universe Books. New York

181017

It seems fitting that a preface to this book of photographs taken in China by Henri Cartier-Bresson in the last days of the Old Regime, and the first weeks of the New, should be written by me while on a visit to China after nearly six years of absence.

I have returned to China, not as a stranger. I was born in Old China, and spent my first twenty years of life in Peking, then the war years in Chungking, and was there once again in 1949 and 1950, about the time when these photographs were taken by Cartier-Bresson. In these pictures, multi-dimensional by reason of their vivid realism, the raw, undiluted despair of a people driven beyond endurance by suffering and misrule, the pent-up fury of a nation overripe for revolution, leap to the unjaded eye and stay in the unprejudiced mind, needing no further explanation. Better than words can ever describe, they proclaim the inevitability of that immense upheaval which is called the Communist Revolution of China.

I too saw the crumbling of the Old China, Kuomintang China rotten from within, helpless and paralyzed by self-corruption. I watched, hesitant and dubious (for like most of us I am afraid of absolute dogmas), the first fine exaltations of the Revolution triumphant. I stood while its processions passed, its drums beat, its flags rippled in the wind of heaven and its songs filled the air. I saw the kindness, the honesty of the soldiers of the Communist armies, contrasting strongly with the looting and destruction of the soldiers of the Kuomintang armies. Fear ebbed; hope returned. Then the frenzies of a people too long oppressed swept the land as the great reforms of the new regime began, demanding justice, deliverance from poverty, freedom from hunger, and an end to corruption.

There was greatness and therefore victory; and in triumph there were also mistakes made. Crimes were committed, in the name of justice and equality, and this was nothing new in the history of the world. But many people in the West, once subject to the same upheavals, are shocked by the turbulent rages of other nations, forgetting that they too underwent the same growing pains, enacted the same errors, were prone to the same sweeping intolerance, decades or even centuries ago. Like all the other revolutions, the Chinese revolution has had its share of spilt blood along with its enormous social reforms. It has perpetrated its tyrannies side by side with its ideas made concrete and enduring. But in these six years of growth and maturing and achievement, hardship and toil and trial and error, it has solidly established the foundations of a New Order which, for 600 million people, has replaced chronic starvation by sufficiency and glaring injustice by peace, full employment, and equal justice for all. For people like myself, who return as observers, and critical observers at that, the overwhelming change is something that cannot be denied or gainsaid. If we can accept, in a casual lapse of imagination, that our standard of living and security of existence should be much higher than that of other peoples; if want and hunger elsewhere than in our own house leave us unmoved; then the photographs of pre-revolution China which Cartier-Bresson has given us will awake no emotion but a nostalgic, wistful yearning for those good old photogenic days full of ragged beggars and putrid slums where tens of thousands lived a less than sardine life, their misery a challenge to our pens and our cameras, but by no means to be shared. The smiles wreathing the faces of children whose corpses would sometimes be found, stone frozen in back alleys, would be a gaiety worth recording, and with no qualms we would say, as has been said before : "But life in the East was always cheap; there are so many of them."

This, however, is no longer true today. All humanity deems itself worthy to partake equally of the wealth of this rich world of ours. Asia is emerging from the nightmare horrors which have plagued her for so long, and they can no longer be wished back upon the people of China, present-day China.

This is the present, as I have seen it, coming by slow train, alone and completely free to go where I please and to do whatever I like.

All the way up from the south, across the red plains of the Yangtse basin, their horizons bordered by blue crested hills; across the northern plains with the meandering Yellow River, once China's sorrow; in all directions were fields, green and fertile, curved and fitted to each other, rich with promise of harvest. But I noticed two new things which had never been before. The first was trees. Everywhere, it seemed, were trees, some larger and some smaller, but all young, and the hills, once so barren, were fuzzy with saplings. The bleak look of the northern plains which I remembered so well had gone, and the good earth waved these green pennants in promise of the future, as far as eye could reach. The second thing was the farmers. I remembered them well, and their rags. But now there were no rags. These people working in the fields all looked as landlords once used to look. They were well dressed, many of them had new clothes on, all of the young men had clean white undershirts. In the north the padded jackets were often new and this not on one back but on hundreds, on thousands of backs. In all the stations it was the same. Everyone without exception was dressed adequately and warmly, and all the children too. The houses were clean, rethatched and repaired, and there were many new houses and completely new villages.   And this was no Potemkin stageplay.   Off the railway tracks, inland, east and west, south and north, it was thus over all of China's land, everywhere.

Where the Yellow River once swept its bronze flood waters at will across land submissive to disaster, and peasants crept on their roof tops to watch and starve, are now dikes, dams, canals, a huge irrigation system, with hundreds of thousands of laborers bent with shovel and pickaxe and small baskets side by side with bulldozers and lorries, toiling as ants do, to keep the fields secure.

Where the loess swaddles its tons of dust about the hills of the Northwest and levels valleys into plateaux, in the arid and semi-desert land once abandoned to the sands of the Gobi, new cities and towns born overnight clamor for houses and schools, cinemas and theaters, libraries and restaurants, shops and railway stations and airfields. The railways and the roads gouge their way toward the center of Asia, the high places once thought impossible to reach, and in this accelerated progress which is Asia in the jet age, already airplanes zoom daily to places still romantic and remote to the rest of the world : Peking to Lhasa, capital of Tibet, is only a day by air. And it takes but four hours from Peking to Ulan Bator, in Inner Mongolia.

To belittle or to ignore the achievement of New China, what has been created and maintained in the past six years, is no longer merely slightly insane, it is positively dangerous.   To hope for inefficiency, to predicate inner disruption, is sheer fantasy. There is no inefficiency, and there is complete, whole-hearted, and enthusiastic support by the people of China for all that has been done.   There is plenty of food, and it is good and cheaper than it has been for twenty years.   There is enough to clothe everyone.   There is more than full employment; in fact, there are hundreds of thousands more jobs to be filled than there are people to fill them.   These are facts and they must be made known.

I know that many people in the United States will feel as I felt before I came here and saw with my own eyes what had been done.   In this rosy picture of success, achievement, buildings going up overnight, thousands toiling away in factories and in the fields, they will see sullen, driven slave labor, compelled to backbreaking toil, and hating the tyranny that lords over them.   They will think of a herded and compliant youth, fanatically imbued with political creed, hastily trained to become cogs in the wheels of a merciless and tyrannical state machine.   It is not so.

There is a compelling enthusiasm, obvious and too genuine not to move and stir one deeply, however critical of its imperfections one may be.   There are thousands *of unselfish and dedicated people to be met in every walk of life, from bus conductors to engineers or school teachers. They work hard because they want to work hard, they are proud of their country and what it has already achieved, and they want it to be more beautiful and a happy place for themselves and for their children. There is laughter and eagerness such as I saw in the faces of the workmen driving long shafts into the river bed where a great new bridge was going to span it. They loved their work, and in their minds already was the vision of the bridge which they spoke of as "our bridge". There is absorption and the joy of discovery in the heads of students bent over microscopes or poring in the libraries, pride and loving care in the microscopes and in the libraries, pride and loving care in the hands of those driving tractors and lorries. This cannot be faked day in and day out, in a hundred places.*

There is more. I had thought that I would meet, as one critic had put it, the blank wall and the polite smile, evading questions, evading argument. I thought that argument would be impossible, because it always is in the presence of fanaticism. But again I was left confused and perplexed by reality. For I found critical minds, outspokenness, and originality. True, there were political controls which would prove rankling to an American mind but they are getting less and less while daily grows the sense of freedom of opinion, of controversy and individual affirmation. And this is no propaganda stunt. It is a natural development from the stable, secure foundations which have been established in New China.

All who love China as I know many Americans do will hope that this progress toward the kind of freedom which the West has deemed so precious so rightly, will grow and become strong. China is moving swiftly ahead, yet with the years her own essential commonsense wisdom and the treasures of her past are becoming more precious and valuable.

There is one other thing which I have noted and that is a complete absence of xenophobia, that anti-white feeling once obvious and prevalent. Going about in many places, on ferries exchanging cigarettes with laborers coming home from work, in railway carriages playing poker with Communist officials, sipping tea in farmhouses or university campuses, everywhere people have said, openly and gladly, how much they wish that the people of the United States could once more be their friends.

I too wish that some of my American friends who love China and wish her well could be here today, watching the magnolias wither as spring turns to summer and the willows stand crestfallen and languid over the pools, and the red walls and golden roofs glow in the sun in Peking, the enchanted city, spellbinding as ever. I wish they could be here along with many other visitors to China, Belgian and French university professors, British businessmen and German technicians, Swiss and Italians, Japanese and Indians and Indonesians and so many others who roam the cities of China, take photographs, sightsee in the parks or, in once famous restaurants, now just as famous and as full, eat Peking duck.

This is what I have seen, though it was not what I expected. I shall quote a Pakistani friend of mine, a deeply anti-Communist young man, who came here a few weeks ago. He and I went strolling last night round the quiet streets of the Forbidden City and he remarked how secure one felt at night in the streets. There were no policemen about, yet one felt as safe as in a house. "I can't explain what has happened to me," he said. "I came to pass judgment, to find fault. I wanted to write a sensation story on China. But I can't do it now. What is being done is too big to be belittled. China's got all the answers; she's learning so fast, she's not going to make the mistakes that have been made elsewhere. And there's nothing fake about all this. We've got to tell it to the world. It's no use trying to put the clock back."

Han Suyin

Peking. June 1956

This book is the diary of a journey in China, a diary kept by a photographer-reporter, for the most part in pictures.

My stay in China, where I went on assignment for Life magazine, lasted eleven months. I lived there for five months under the Kuomintang government. I witnessed the first six months of the present regime.

At the beginning of December 1948 I went by air from Rangoon to China. I was thus able to reach Peking twelve days before it was taken by Mao Tse-tung's troops. I left the capital by the last aircraft to leave the city before the Communists arrived.

After landing in Shanghai I sought means to get into the zones controlled by the People's Army. I crossed the line near Tsing-Tao in the Shan-tung peninsula. I had been told that missionaries had no difficulty in using this route to get back to their missions. Why not follow their example, pushing my luggage before me on a hand-cart? I was about to take that course when I met a journalist and a businessman who proposed to go the same way, but in a jeep. We set off together,

taking our chance. Owing to the snow of the 1948-1949 winter we had trouble in distinguishing roads from fields. When we got near to the lines I went forward on foot, waving a white handkerchief on the end of a stick and likewise my French passport, our best safeguard in that white and rather nerve-racking solitude.

After covering eight miles in this style we reached a village where a detachment of the People's Army was billeted. The soldiers consi-dered our trek across no-man's-land very unwise. We had not been invited into their zone and were certainly not expected. We were unable to continue our journey. We spent five very inte-resting weeks in one of the village farms. After which we resigned ourselves to returning to Shanghai. I have given this account in some detail because, obviously, I was unable to bring back any photographs, and this description is therefore necessary to complete my picture diary.

Back in Shanghai I found the city completely disorganized. I left it, in the company of a party of Buddhists making a pilgrimage for peace to the sanctuaries of Hangchow. There I heard that the front was rapidly approaching the Yangtze.

I hastened to Nanking, reaching that city, the Kuomintang capital, by the last train in. There I witnessed the departure of Chiang K'ai-shek's last supporters and the arrival of the People's Army. They allowed me to continue as a photo-grapher, the law permitting foreigners to practise their trades, but I had, of course, to cope with all the difficulties inherent in war conditions.

I stayed in Nanking from April to July 1949. I then went to Shanghai for the third time and there, since my last visit, the popular forces had taken over the government.

At the beginning of autumn a ship arrived to take off such foreigners as wished to leave. I put myself down as a passenger. Before leaving I had to submit all my most recent photographs for censorship. None of the pictures raised great objections though I had endless discussions with the censor. I went on board at the end of September 1949 and disembarked in the great English port of Hong-Kong some days later. And there my Chinese journey and my photographic diary ended.

Henri Cartier-Bresson.

1. *About eight days before the departure of the Kuomintang troops and the arrival of the People's Army, life in Peking goes on peacefully. A street trader is delighted to meet a friend who has just bought a length of cotton material. Respect, benevolence and calm, virtues which the Chinese are unwilling to lose in any circumstances, are practised on the eve of one of the greatest changes in China's long history.*

2. *In the Forbidden City. A solitary pedestrian, perhaps an ex-official, thinking of the events which everyone is expecting.*

3. This eunuch was in the service of the Dowager Empress Tsz'e Hsi, who died in 1909. The Imperial household included four hundred eunuchs, chamberlains of the princes of the blood, of the emperors, and of their concubines. All the other Imperial servants were women. In 1949 about forty of these eunuchs were still living in a monastery near Peking.

3

4

6

5

4. 5. 6. *The Tai-miao gardens, temple of the Imperial ancestors, near the former Palace of the Emperors. Every morning at dawn, and even earlier, men came to practise sabre exercises and to do Chinese gymnastics. The movements have a spiritual or mental as well as a physical object, and are designed to give mastery of both mind and body. Among these men are a museum curator, a bank clerk and a Kuomintang officer who, despite the nearness of the fighting, regularly did two hours of these quasi-ritual exercises.*

8

7. Nanking, for long the Kuomintang capital, still has the old city walls, longer than those of any other Chinese town. They have survived a number of dynasties and the T'ai-ping peasant revolt. Here a section is seen reflected in the lake where the Ming navy did its training in the fourteenth century. These people are collecting lotus roots for fuel.

8. Craftsmen polishing jade, as precious to the Chinese as are diamonds to Europeans. Their workshop is full of a good smell of cabbage and the family cooking.

9. Booksellers of the Peking " flea-market ". A gramophone plays an old Viennese waltz while collectors search for rare books. Peking has been one of the principal cultural centers of the world for many centuries.

9

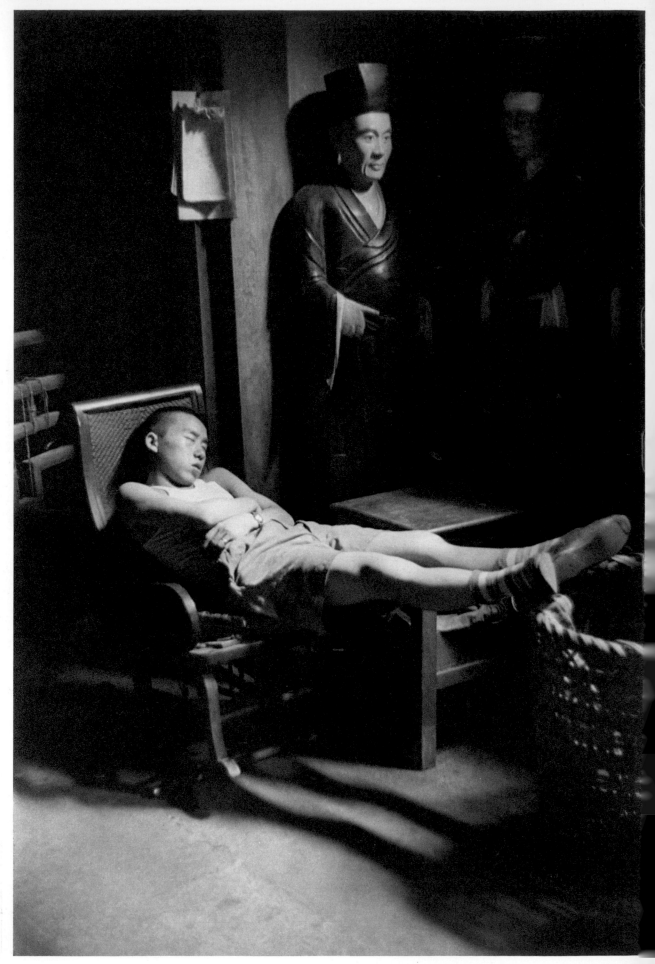

10. *At Shanghai, in the temple of Nan-tao. The watchman has fallen asleep in the shadow of his idols.*

11. *One pilgrim burns incense, while others take refreshment; the father of the family seems to appreciate the excellent vegetarian meals which are served in the temples.*

12. A Shanghai hawker. He sells peanuts and Chinese cigarettes—more or less successful fakes of foreign brands. Behind him is a book-shop in the window of which are portraits of Marshal Chiang K'ai-shek and of Sun Yat-sen together with a phrase from the latter's writings : " The Revolution is not over, my companions will have to continue it ." In front of his portrait, four marriage-certificate rolls.

13. At Peking, Lu Li-chang, in the street of the antiquaries and booksellers. The children of a paint-brush merchant. True Chinese writing is drawn with such a brush. The large brushes are for drawing the characters, over a yard square, used in shop signs.

14. Tea-house in Peking, where the customers come with their cage-birds.

15. *The day's trading over, a peasant who has come to Peking to sell his vegetables, sits down to eat his provisions, a Chinese loaf and a gruel of cereals. The shopkeeper seems resigned to having nothing left in his shop to sell. Peking has already been entered by the People's Armies.*

12

13

14

16

17

16. Under the Pai-lo arches in one of Peking's principal streets. People stop to eat hot soup sold by open-air cooks.

17. At Hangchow. Coolies resting between two rickshaw jobs. Marco Polo visited Hangchow in the thirteenth century and left a famous description of this former capital of the Sung dynasty (960-1280). There is a Chinese proverb which says, " Above is Paradise, below are Hangchow and Suchow."

18. At Shanghai in the chapel of the Goddess of Mercy in the Nan-tao quarter. A basket-maker's family at lunch.

19

19. 20. *The Shanghai bridges are hump-backed. Children wait about at them for hand-carts and rickshaws, and help to push. Then they run after the rickshaws for payment, although often their help has not been asked for. Shanghai is dominated by skyscrapers. The three highest floors of this one were occupied by the foreign press club, where foreign correspondents from overseas lived. Foreign, civil and military administrations had their offices in the rest of the building.*

21. *At Nanking, the bazaar of the temple of Confucius (Fu-Tse-miao). Two young barbers at work. A fortune-teller predicting the future for a Kuomintang policeman.*

22

22. A blind man, led by a child whom he keeps on a leash. The old Imperial paving is longer lived than the concrete sidewalks laid by the municipality under the Kuomintang.

23. A beggar-woman and her child outside a Moslem restaurant. The paper in front of her reads : " My name is Sun. My husband died of a sickness. He left this child, and myself, his widow, behind him. Here we are in a strange city. We have no means of livelihood. I am thus forced to ask charity of the good-hearted."

24. The siesta hour in a shop which rents out Mah-jong sets. Posters advertise Sword cigarettes and Champion spark-plugs.

25. A street-trader and his son.

26. This photographer also sells ceremonial clothes, advertised by neon letters. Below the shop-sign his goods are advertised in the following terms : " My ceremonial garments, the very latest, are very precious. You will give me pleasure if you come in and try them on. My prices are very reasonable."

27. 28. *In the Chi-Ho-lu suburb of Peking. But the scene could just as well be in any Chinese city. Men, women and children rummage untiringly among the city rubbish dumps, to recover all sorts of objects. The dogs wait behind them, anxiously hoping that something will be left for them to eat.*

27

28

30

29

31

29. 30. 31. *On the Bund in Shanghai. On the avenue beside the river are banks, customs offices, and the head offices of great companies. Here ships are unloaded. As soon as any bales of cotton are landed on the wharfs by the coolies, they are besieged by beggars. They tear out handfuls of cotton, to sell or to line their clothes. A watchman gives them a tap with his stick, without hurting them much, and they soon return to start again.*

32

32. *The body of a baby girl, abandoned by her family on the pavement, wrapped in red cotton padding. Later on, the municipal services will take away the poor creature, dead from hunger and exposure during the bitterly cold nights.*

33. *" The little teachers " belong to an organization founded by Mrs. Sun Yat-sen. They are taught to read a few of the commoner characters, which they undertake to teach, in their turn, to other children or adults. Eighty-five per cent of the Chinese population were illiterate. Primary schools teach 1,000 characters. A newspaper uses 2,500. A well-educated man knows at least 10,000.*

34. *" The little teachers " learning and interpreting a mimed song.*

35. *The same children waiting for a distribution of rice. They are gentle and polite, but their faces reflect the sadness of centuries of suffering.*

33

34

From day to day

36. *General Ma Hung-kwei came to Nanking, Kuomintang capital, every year to meet Marshal Chiang K'ai-shek. The first syllable of his name, Ma, means horse, a very common designation among Chinese Moslems. Behind him, carefully written, are some old rhymed precepts : " A good general should occupy a splendid place in history. He should be praised during a hundred generations. He should be full of care for his men and also for his people." General Ma was the big war lord of Northwest China. His secretaries were dressed as hospital nurses. He adored ice-cream and always had bucketfuls handy, and offered it to his guests. Shortly after this photograph was taken, General Ma was abandoned by his troops.*

37. *The last session of the Nationalist parliament at Nanking. Some months previously the deputies had re-elected Marshal Chiang K'ai-shek President of the Republic for a further six years.*

38. *The Nationalist general Yen Shi-san, one of the most famous of the war lords and absolute master of Shansi province from 1909 until 1949. General Yen is now in Formosa.*

37

38

39. 40. Peking. Reading the newspaper. The headlines announce good news : " The Nationalist armies are advancing toward the South and gaining important successes. " On the same day the Communists reached the city gates.

41. Eight o'clock in the morning at the Imperial Palace in Peking. Ten thousand recruits, mobilized principally from the ranks of small traders, line up to form a new Nationalist regiment.

42. Out of the ten thousand recruits, three thousand have received uniforms and been brigaded. Anxious parents look for their sons among these new soldiers.

43. Peking. Kuomintang cavalry, on their little Mongol horses, on the periphery of the airport.

39

40

43

44

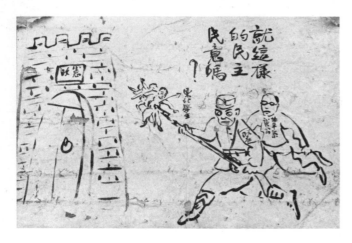

45

46

47

44. *The suburbs of Peking. A marriage procession going toward the outskirts. The bride
is in a carefully closed palanquin and is surrounded
by the men of her family. The drummers at the
head of the procession are wearing a costume
which belongs to the last Imperial period. The
procession stops in front of the bridegroom's house.
Going in the other direction, retreating Kuomintang
troops make for the city center. The two processions seem completely alien to each other.*

45. 46. *The Peking National Library. The young
men are refugee students. An anti-Kuomintang
poster says: " Is that democracy ? " Most of the
students were against the Kuomintang.*

47. *Nanking. The last days of the Kuomintang.
Nationalist soldiers killing time in a little suburban
menagerie. Boredom, waiting, indecision. The
atmosphere is the same as it was in Peking in
the week before the fall of the city.*

48. *Shanghai. The banks of the Hwang-pu.*
Until 1937 the park was " forbidden to Chinese
and dogs ''. When the city fell to the Japanese
in 1937, any white man passing this point was forced
to bow his head. Chinese junks have remained
unchanged for many centuries. The warship is
American. From the mid-nineteenth century on,
the British admiral's flagship was traditionally
anchored at this spot.

49. On the Shanghai Bund. Galloping inflation makes a coffin a good investment for those holding paper money. The coolies haul at it while singing a melancholy kind of chantey.

50. Nanking, on the south bank of the Yangtze. Refugee peasants from the North hope to cross the river by boarding junks, and so return home. The other side of the river was already held by the People's Armies, who themselves crossed the river to the south bank a week later.

48

49

51

51. *Hangchow. March 29th, in the new moon, an anniversary commemorating the seventy-two martyrs of the Sun Yat-sen revolution. Pilgrims crowding to an expiatory temple built by the emperor in memory of General Yo-fei, after he had been unjustly executed as a traitor. The faithful pray for peace, caressing eleventh-century idols to persuade them to intercede for them.*

52. *A Kuomintang soldier burning incense so that his wishes may be granted.*

53. *For several centuries pilgrims have come to the temple of Yo-fei, to spit on the iron statues of two traitors.*

54. *Buddhist monks, before the statues of their gods, pray for peace for hours at a stretch.*

52

53

55. *At every street corner speculators buy and sell silver dollars for paper money.*

56. 57. *Shanghai, December 1948. The gold rush. Enormous lines form outside the banks, on the Bund, and overflow into neighboring streets, dislocating all traffic. About ten people were crushed or trampled to death. The Kuomintang had decided to distribute some of the gold reserve, at the rate of 1 1/2 ounces per head. Some people waited more than twenty-four hours, trying to get rid of paper money. Order was more or less maintained by oldsiers equiped with odds and ends deriving from all the various armies which, in the past fifteen years, have played a part in Chinese history.*

58. 59. 60. A large number of different articles were lost in the crush. The street cleaners filled whole carts with broken umbrellas and other nondescript objects. Some preferred to give up and leave the queue, carrying whatever booty they could pick up in the streets; others, one hand clinging to the wall so as to keep their place, continued to wait their turn to get gold.

61. Shanghai is besieged by the Communists. All traffic on Suchow canal brought to a stop by the sampans tying up at the city. Shouts and arguments, but no fighting. In China, he who strikes the first blow is always in the wrong.

58

59

62

63

62. The front has now reached the suburbs of Shanghai. An every-man-for-himself flight from the city begins. Small ships leave the Bund piers.

63. High officials about to take off by plane for Formosa. The tennis racket looks more like a holiday departure.

64. Waiting outside Shanghai railway station.

65

66

67

68

65. 66. 67. 68. At Nanking. People save such household articles as they can, and get away as best they can, even crammed into vehicles similar to the horse-drawn buggies of 1900.

69. Nanking railway station. A Nationalist soldier rocking his baby to sleep.

70. The station is full of refugee peasants, lying on the ground. There have been no trains for several days.

71. 72. The endless flow of retreating soldiers
across Nanking. They are making south, every
man for himself.

73. 74. At Nanking. The Kuomintang authorities
have abandoned their capital, but the People's
Army was not to arrive for forty-eight hours.
During the lull, the usual life of the city came to a
standstill and food grew scarce. Military food
and clothing stores were raided for rice, blankets
and some cotton fabrics.

71

72

75

76

75. 76. *Floorboards taken from the abandoned villa of a high official to make fuel for cooking rice. Only the barest necessities were looted. The Chinese poor have a keen sense of property. The foreign colony was fearful of destruction, large-scale looting and acts of violence. Nothing of the kind occurred during the interregnum.*

77. The interregnum has now lasted more than forty hours. There is shooting in the streets more or less everywhere, but the shots cause practically no excitement.

78. At the entrance to the National Library, students of Nanking hoist a banner panel— " Welcome to the army of liberation ".

79. Meanwhile some of the people are still taking advantage of the fact that the rice shops are abandoned, to help make up for the scarcity of foodstuffs.

77

78

The interregnum

80. *Students have stuck up posters painted during the last days of the Kuomintang which represented their views on the annihilation of the Kuomintang army, the confiscation of Chiang K'ai-chek's money, and the crushing of his intrigues.*

81. *The population gathers to greet the People's Army on the great square of Nanking, before the statue of Sun Yat-sen.*

82. *Students writing the words of a song on a wall. The tune is given in the form of figures.*

81

82

83

84

83. A police corps is organized by volunteers.

84. The first soldiers of the People's Army arriving in Nanking on foot. They are cheered, but at the same time regarded with a good deal of anxious curiosity. In China, a soldier has always been considered a looter, living off the country, for which reason the military profession is greatly despised.

85. The soldiers of the new army have a somewhat rudimentary equipment. They sing their three Orders: 1. Don't steal even a needle and thread. 2. Consider the people as your own family. 3. Whatever you may have borrowed, return it.

86. The population of Nanking still regards the newcomers with great curiosity, the more so since these soldiers from the North do not speak the same dialect. The white bags, worn by the troops in the form of a bandolier, contain their rice ration. On their backs they carry everything necessary for their subsistence.

88

87. *The peasant-soldiers take shelter from the torrid heat of the Shanghai summer in the shadow of the skyscrapers where they are billeted. Shanghai has a larger population than Paris and is the fifth most populous city in the world.*

88. *Nanking. A Nationalist officer prisoner in a rickshaw. Beside him, a soldier of the People's Army carrying the weapons which have been taken from the officer.*

89. *These Northern soldiers do not speak the language of Nanking, but Chinese writing is understood all over China whatever the dialect spoken. To make themselves understood the newcomers draw characters in the palm of their hand. A literate man is always considered to be a superior person, and a fountain-pen is to some extent the mark of the literate.*

90. *The soldiers of the People's Army were almost all peasants. They had never seen refrigerators and were surprised at the sight of them in Shanghai.*

89

90

94

98

99

100

98. Satirical contemporary theater. A peasant and a workman explain what Chiang K'ai-shek, his wife and friends really are. The latter are represented by other actors who caricature them.

99. Chinese opera. Actors representing a king and queen singing in front of a gigantic portrait of Mao Tse-tung. The People's Army organized numerous stage performances. The Chinese public is very fond of opera. Traditional style was respected, but in some cases the action of the piece was modified by the Government whenever it was considered reactionary.

100. Court of popular justice at Shanghai. The judge explains his sentence to the public, since the new code of laws has not yet been published.

101. *Shanghai, July 7, 1949. Celebrating the liberation. Meeting at the Grand Theater. General Chen-yi, Military Governor of the city, standing before a portrait of the C.-in-C. Chu-teh. General Chen-yi was one of Mao Tse-tung's first disciples. Before that he spent some time in France, as a student and as a worker in the Renault factory. During the Long March, Chen-yi was left behind to organize resistance and partisans* in Kiangsi province, which was reoccupied by Chiang K'ai-shek.

102. *In the front row of the audience, Mrs. Chou En-Lai and Mrs. Sun Yat-Sen. Mrs. Chou En-Lai made the journey from Peking to pay the new regime's respects to the widow of the leader of the 1911 revolution.*

101

102

103

103. 105. *Parade of athletes at the Soviet Club before the archdeacon of the Russian Orthodox Church at Shanghai.*

104. *Reception July 14, 1949, at the French Consulate.*

106. *Reception at the British Consulate. All the great Powers were represented at Shanghai, which was a very international city. Businessmen wonder what the future holds for them.*

104

107. 108. 110. After the taking of Shanghai there were so many parades and meetings that they almost overlapped. Here is the celebration of the official entry of the army into Shanghai on August 1, 1949. A Union delegate holds an enlarged copy of the new paper money. The processions were used to publicize problems of the hour. The ceremony had been planned for July 5 but in the face of the Kuomintang threat to bomb it from the air, it was postponed to the 6th.

109. *The Trade Unions joined in the processions. Post Office workers carrying a telephone dial, emblem of their trade. The inscriptions are not written in Chinese, that language only having become the official language of the city again quite recently.*

111. *Students of the Protestant American University in a people's procession at Nanking. A banner announces that the People's Army will soon take Canton, provisional capital of the Kuomintang.*

109

110

112. *The banner is directed against " Bureaucratic capitalism, feudalism and imperialism ".*

113. *In the same procession, portrait of General Chu-teh.*

114. *Political fancy-dress in a parade. The clown is holding a fan bearing the inscription " Refuse the silver dollar " (Kuomintang currency). The other young man is covered with worthless paper money, symbolizing inflation. On his back he wears the white sun on a blue background, emblem of the Kuomintang, and the names of the four " great families ", principal financiers and supporters of Chiang K'ai-shek, the Changs, Soongs, Kungs and Chens.*

115. *At Shanghai the Pu-tong dockers feature the traditional Chinese dragon, which has appeared in all Chinese celebrations for thousands of years, in the procession.*

111

112

116. 118. *The Yao-ku, peasant dance in stylized costume, and always accompanied by tambourines. Here it is being danced by an army theater group.*

117. *Students dancing the Yanko in a procession. It is a Northern spring dance, sung and danced by the peasants at the time of sowing the seed. The Yanko was adopted by the Army, and was carried by the troops to all parts of the country. Its popularity was extraordinary, so much so that many products were named after it because of its publicity value.*

119. *For the festivities the streetcars were decorated by the employees to celebrate the liberation. The streetcar company of Shanghai was formerly French.*

120. *Traditional characters of Chinese opera take part in the procession. They can be distinguished by their stylized make-up. The white paint round the eyes of a character signifies that he is both ill-natured and ridiculous.*

116

117

121. *Procession of students demonstrating against the black market. The procession passed along the Shanghai Bund. Behind them, the skyscraper of the Soong Bank, the greatest financial house in China.*

122. *The banner bears the inscription " Let us work for the people's happiness ". The " Pointed Nose " represents, in China, the white man. He is followed by his servants, in dog and falcon masks.*

123. *Numerous tanks bring up the rear of a military procession. They are of American manufacture and were captured from the Nationalists.*

124. *Shanghai, Nanking Road. Before the race-course: a Trade Union procession going one way, the Army the other.*

122

123

126

125. 126. 127. People's Army holiday in the French park, at Shanghai, which lasted six days. Stage and screen stars signed fans and also took part in shows which were watched, every day, by thirty thousand spectators. In Shanghai, most actors were Left-wing and reportedly held aloof from the Kuomintang shows.

128. Portrait-painter's shop, Shanghai, in the Nan-tao quarter. These artists work either from nature or from a photograph. The window display includes portraits of ancestors, of a famous comic actor, of the former mayor of Shanghai, K. V. Wu, and a plump baby. An up-to-date novelty, a portrait of Mao Tse-tung.

129. A poster with two slogans: " Increase production; Make our economy prosperous ".

130. The cultural department of the People's Army installs libraries everywhere (novels, illustrated albums, political pamphlets, etc.) and also exhibitions. Soldiers of the People's Army visiting an exhibition of paintings representing a typical range of subjects : they cover the country's poverty, and the union between peasants and soldiers.

127

131. *Traveling library at Shanghai. Children are very good customers, and the new government is publishing illustrated story-books for them.*

132. *Shanghai, September 1949. Performance of a satirical play, "Promotion". This scene shows Marshal Chiang K'ai-shek, furious at his military reverses, reproaching his brother-in-law, H. H. Kung, the great financier and Minister of Finance. The play was written under the Kuo-mintang government, but the version produced at that time was naturally much less outspoken.*

133. *At the People's Army theater, performance of a play adapted from " The Pilgrim Monkey ". This novel, by Wu-cheng, is the masterpiece of Chinese sixteenth-century literature.*

134. *A People's Army theater group performing the popular peasant dance called Yanko.*

135. *Forty centuries of life in China.*

132

133

134

Departure

136. After a five-months blockade, an American ship dropped anchor in Shanghai harbor to take off foreigners wishing to leave the city.

139

137

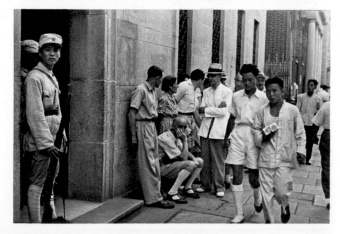

138

137. 138. *Before granting an exit visa the authorities required foreigners to advertise their departure in two newspapers, one English and the other
Chinese, to inform possible creditors and thus
prevent them leaving the country without paying
their debts. They are lining up here at police
headquarters waiting for their visas.*

139. *The last rickshaw trip—to the ship which is
to take off foreigners.*

140. *On the dockside. Going aboard.*

141. *Aboard ship. A group of Europeans and
Americans who had long been resident in Shanghai.*

142. *Arriving at Hong-Kong.*

143. *Disembarking at Hong-Kong in British territory.*

144. *Hong-Kong Chinese Traders' Newspaper publishes a special edition with two items of news: All southern China is in the hands of the People's Army; and a Political Consultative Assembly has met in Peking to give a new constitution to millions of Chinese.*

142

143

Legends of the Remote Past

Chinese civilization arose in the valley of the Hwang-ho, the " Yellow River ", and in the valley of the Wei-ho, one of its tributaries. There the early legendary emperors ruled over the people as divinely appointed sovereigns. One emperor is credited with teaching the people how to till the soil, another with inventing the pictographic script of Chinese writing. A third, Hwang-ti, the " Yellow Emperor " (ca. 2700 B. C.), invented the compass and an early type of combat tank; it was he who unified China and subdued the neighboring savages who threatened to overrun the empire. The empress, Hwang-ti's wife, taught the people to cultivate the mulberry tree for its silkworms. This was China's Golden Age : the men worked the fields, the women wove silk and textiles at home, neighbors loved and succored one another, children were cherished, old folk were venerated, and every man clung to his land, to his garden, to his mulberry trees, to the tomb of his ancestors. The people sang the three-line poem that is still sung today by the Chinese peasant after four millennia of history :

When the sun rises, I go to work,
When the sun sets, I go to rest,
What use is the imperial power to me?

Though it is doubtful whether he ever really existed, Hwang-ti is revered by the Chinese, who still pride themselves on being his descendents. What is supposed to be his tomb is on a mountain between the Yellow River and the Wei-ho. In the past one of the highest officials in the land was sent out each year on the anniversary of his death to pay homage to him there.

After Hwang-ti reigned the three philosopher kings, each a man of the people. Each was also a sage and freely chose his successor as the man most capable of governing wisely. As it so happened, the son of the third philosopher king was a youth of exceptional merit to whom, at the people's insistence, his father passed the reins of government.

Thus was the first hereditary dynasty founded that of the Chous (1050-221 B. C.), with which the recorded history of China begins. The seat of its power, located at first on the river Wei (Shensi province), was later shifted eastward to the Yellow River valley (Honan province); its capital was first Sian, then Loyang. But this was China's feudal age and the history of the Chou dynasty is a long catalogue of clashes between the overlords of the states of Ts'in, Tsin, Lu and Tsi, each of whom wielded more power than the emperor. Yet even in this chaotic period, scholars and artists formed a privileged class apart from the peasantry and the feudal aristocracy, and Chinese culture thrived. Two of the greatest names are Lao-Tse (604-515 B. C.) and Confucius (551-479 B. C.), contemporaries of Socrates and Plato. Each, after his death, inspired a religion in his name.

Confucianism can hardly be called a religion in the Christian sense of the word, as it involves neither theology not clergy nor hierarchy. Confucius himself never bothered his disciples with metaphysical problems. All he asked of them was to be charitable to the poor, respectful to their superiors and honest with themselves. When a man is human-hearted, he said, his example will be followed by other members of his family, and the example of his family will be followed by other families; on this depends a nation's welfare. All office-holders in China were required to be familiar with the Confucian precepts.

Taoism, the system of Lao-Tse, developed simultaneously. Buddhism did not enter the field until about the year 60 A.D., when it was imported from India. But the Chinese are too rational-minded a people for the co-existence of three religions to engender any strife or bloodshed, and in due time, in the 13th century, they coalesced into a single religion with neo-Confucianism as the dominant element.

It was Shi-Hwang-ti, the first "Universal Emperor", who, beginning as king of the state of Ts'in, extended his empire to limits approximating those of modern China. He relegated the Mongol nomads to the Gobi Desert, conceived and built the Great Wall of China, laid out a vast network of roads, standardized money and writing. Resolved to break with the past, he burnt many books and put many scholars and intellectuals to death for "seditious thinking". Discontent followed and after his death (210 B. C.) a rebellion broke out. One of its leaders proclaimed himself emperor and founded a new line. This was the Han dynasty (202 B. C.-200 A. D.), in many ways comparable to the Roman Empire, its contemporary. It was an age of prosperity, of thriving trade and culture, of military expansion (into Central Asia as far as Russian Turkestan, into Korea as far as Seoul, into Indochina as far as Hué).

Then came four centuries of political chaos and fiercely divided interests. Yet now were produced the masterpieces of Buddhist sculpture. The Yangtze Valley, the rice bowl of China, became a key factor in the country's economic life. Nanking developed into the brilliant capital of southern China. Between the Yellow River (Hwang-ho) and the Yangtze was dug the Grand Canal, which for 14 centuries has been the main north-south waterway of inland China.

The T'ang dynasty (618-960) welded the empire together again and ushered in a new period of peace and prosperity, during which art and literature flourished; this was the classical age of Chinese poetry. Under the Sung dynasty (960-1280) came the classical age of Chinese painting. From the mid-12th century on, the Sung ruled only over southern China. In 1213 the Mongol chief-

tain Jenghiz Khan swept over northern China. Then began a period of foreign domination, culminating in 1280 when the great Mongol prince Kublai Khan became Emperor of China and founded the so-called Yuen dynasty (1280-1367). He erected a new capital which he made one of the richest and handsomest cities in the world : this was Peking, known in medieval Europe as Cambaluc. It was in the time of Kublai Khan that Marco Polo appeared in China (1275), where he remained as a trusted friend and familiar of the " Great Khan " for nearly 20 years; in his account of his travels he glowingly describes the wonders of Cambaluc and of Hangchow, the old Sung capital. But from the strictly cultural point of view something of a decadence had set in; the burden of tradition weighed heavy on arts and letters, and that power of continual renewal which had so often revitalized Chinese civilization seemed to be on the wane.

Finally the Mongol emperors were overthrown and replaced by the native Ming dynasty (1367-1644). In the 15th century, in the heart of Peking, a Ming emperor established the " Imperial City " and in the heart of that, the " Forbidden City " enclosed by ramparts, where the emperor's palace stands. From then to now, Peking has been the usual capital of China.

From 1644 to 1911 China again fell under foreign domination, that of the Manchus, who founded the T'sing dynasty. Their empire prospered till the end of the 18th century, extending its rule over Indochina, Burma, Nepal, Tibet and Korea. But bad times stood ahead. The emperors became increasingly corrupt and incompetent. The great seaports fell one by one into the hands of the European powers. China became a playground for pirates, cut-throats and unscrupulous adventurers of every description.

Foreign Intervention in China

Up to the 19th century the Chinese knew next to nothing of life beyond their own frontiers. Cut off from the outside world by vast deserts on the north and west, by the Tibetan plateau on the south, by the Pacific Ocean on the east, and above all isolated in time by age-old traditions, they lived with a sense of complete security. Arrogant out of ignorance, they felt no respect for foreigners; they regarded Europeans and Americans as barbarians and referred to them as " foreign devils ", " big noses " and the like.

The Portuguese had established a trading colony at Macao (near Canton) in the mid-16th century. English merchants first appeared at Canton in the last years of the Ming dynasty, and there, late in the 18th century, a considerable volume of foreign trade was being carried on, chiefly by the British, the Portuguese and the Dutch. The result was that a new era — and anything but a happy one — had opened for China by the first decades of the 19th century, as she found herself compelled to grant concessions to the Western nations. Gradually her doors opened to foreigners and in time

a psychological change came about; as the outsiders, true to the ways of an imperialist era, increased their commercial privileges and imposed their will by force, the arrogance and pride of the Chinese turned to humility, masking behind it a queer mixture of cunning and docility.

Many Chinese shrewdly took advantage of the situation, offering their services to the Europeans to the detriment of their countrymen. These were the compradors, the middlemen of the seaports, the paid agents of foreign commercial interests, many of them converts to Christianity. Frequently dealing more crudely and cruelly with their countrymen than the Europeans did, they thought it clever to speak only English, French or German and to ignore their own language. Describing the China of those days, Sun Yat-sen wrote : " China is not a colony. The mother country feels some sense of moral and material responsibility toward a colony, whereas China is exploited by all and slighted by all ".

Opium-smuggling, overtly carried on for years (despite the reiterated protests of local mandarins) by British merchants at Canton who imported the drug from India, finally goaded the Chinese into war (1840). But they were no match for the British fleet which easily put down all opposition. By the treaty of Nanking (1842) the ports of Amoy, Shanghai, Ningpo and Fuchow, in addition to Canton, were thrown open to foreign trade and Hong-Kong was ceded outright to Great Britain. The lucrative business of opium-smuggling thereupon began afresh and continued unabated. In 1844 Caleb Cushing, United States commissioner in China, negotiated the first American trade concessions from the Manchu empire. Foreign interests prospered all along the line, while the Chinese people languished in abject poverty and had no say in the matter.

Widespread dissatisfaction with the Manchu regime finally led to a peasant uprising known as the T'ai-ping rebellion (1853). A leader came forward in the person of a Christian convert, Hung Siu-ts'üan, who proclaimed himself to be a divine emissary and assumed the title of T'ien Wang or " Heavenly King ". He raised a large army in Kwangsi province and so weak were the Manchu emperors that he was able to conquer two-thirds of China, striking as far north as Tientsin. He was on the verge of occupying Peking and dethroning the Manchu dynasty when the latter sent out against him an army trained and headed by a British officer, Major Charles George Gordon, which in 1864 crushed the T'ai-ping rebels. T'ien Wang committed suicide and thousands of his followers were put to the sword.

For the rest of the 19th century the Manchu dynasty was personified by the dowager empress Tsz'e Hsi, a vain, cruel woamn of consuming ambition who had risen from the position of imperial concubine to one of unchallenged power. She did little good to China and incalculable harm. The situation was only aggravated by the rise of a ruthlessly militaristic Japan, which stopped at nothing in her methodical attempts to exploit and demoralize the Chinese people. In utter contempt of Chinese law, the Japanese established opium dens and houses of prostitution by the thousands on Chinese soil. Victor in her wars against China (1894-1895) and Russia (1904-1905), Japan took control of Korea and Manchuria, and now laid plans for occupying the whole of China.

Meanwhile, in 1900-1901, the Boxer rebellion, a very violent anti-foreign movement, had taken place. The Manchu government was either unable or unwilling to check the outbreak. All the foreign legations in Peking were burnt down or besieged, with much loss of life, and the city was even cut off from the world for six weeks. Finally an international army moved in and order was restored.

Dr. Sun Yat-sen, born in 1866 near Canton, was one of the first Chinese to take active steps against the poverty and abasement of his country. He launched the political party known as the Kuomintang (which means " nationalist party ") to which the younger generation of Chinese enthusiastically adhered. He founded schools to contend against illiteracy and published newspapers to inform the people of what was going on both in their own country and in the world at large. Outbreaks against the imperial authorities began to occur and thousands of young revolutionaries were executed by the Manchu government. But there was no quenching the flame that had flared up. By 1911 all southern China was clamoring for the abdication of the Manchus. The all-powerful dowager empress Tsz'e Hsi had died in 1909 and the Emperor Pu-yi was but a child of five. The majority of political and military leaders at Peking sided with Sun Yat-sen. The child ruler was deposed and Sun Yat-sen elected president of a republic. But the time was not ripe; the privileged classes forced him to resign and he returned to Canton, predicting that the Revolution would nevertheless run its course.

After his departure, the generals in Peking, the so-called " war lords ", jockeyed for position and vied for power. Each had an army and a province of his own; each ingratiated himself with a foreign government which supplied him with advisors and arms. In his own province each general ruled supreme, levying taxes and battening on his " subjects ". It was not unusual for taxes to be collected not merely annually, but for years in advance; for example, in 1920 the peasants of Szechwan province had already paid their taxes up to the year 2000, eighty years in advance ! Should a peasant be found penniless, his fate depended on the mood of the tax-collectors; his house could be burnt or confiscated, his oxen carried off, his daughters violated, he himself could be shot pitilessly. The only rule of life in countless districts of China was a squalid poverty, helplessness and backwardness such as no American or European can conceive of without having seen it with his own eyes.

In 1919 the Chinese Communist party was founded at Shanghai; Mao Tse-tung was one of the founding members. Its chief aim coincided with that of Sun Yat-sen and the Kuomintang :

break the iron grip of foreign interests on the coast and the iron grip of the feudal war lords in the interior. In 1923 Sun Yat-sen organized a revolutionary Kuomintang government at Canton in cooperation with the Communists and with the active support of Russia. The leading light of Sun's entourage was a young officer named Chiang K'ai-shek, who was put in charge of the army. Several high cabinet posts were held by Communists, the Ministry of the Peasantry being assigned to Mao Tse-tung, a specialist in agricultural problems.

In 1925 Sun Yat-sen died; his position at the head of the Canton government and the Kuomintang was inherited by Chiang K'ai-shek. In 1926 he led the revolutionary armies in their famous Northern March from Canton through the Yangtze Valley to Nanking, breaking the power of the war lords as they went. China seethed with revolution. Foreign businessmen feared not only for their profitable concessions but for their very lives. Chiang and his armies arrived triumphantly in Shanghai in February 1927. Almost at once he came to terms with the foreign interests in China and they were left unmolested. Next, without a word of warning, Chiang broke the revolutionary alliance of Communists and Kuomintang, carried out wholesale executions of political prisoners, and drove the Communist party underground.

Led by Mao Tse-tung and Chu-teh, the Communists withdrew to the mountains of Kiangsi province, in central China, where they formed a government and set themselves in opposition to the Kuomintang.

Chiang K'ai-shek married into the fabulous Soong family, one of the wealthiest in China. He had reunited China, but at the price of renouncing agrarian reform and the betterment of the working classes, for his support came from the industrial and commercial aristocracy and the landed gentry. Nanking was made the new capital. The Kuomintang government was recognized all over the world. Chiang's prestige was at its peak.

In 1932 Chiang mobilized his armies and encircled the Communist-held zones of Kiangsi. But the main body of the Communist forces, with whom the peasants were in sympathy, managed to break through and by 1935, after an epic march of 6000 miles, they had entrenched themselves in northwest China, in Shensi province.

Taking advantage of this civil war, the Japanese moved in and occupied Manchuria in 1932. Five years later they invaded the Peking and Shanghai regions. From then on, total war devastated China from end to end ; it cost the Japanese three million lives and the Chinese many more, exact figures being indeterminable.

With the threat of Japanese conquest hanging over China, the Kuomintang and the Communists again joined forces. The Communist armies were merged with the nationalist armies; Chiang K'ai-shek was recognized as commander-in-chief of both. The Kuomintang government withdrew to Chungking accompanied by a permanent Communist delegation headed by Chou En-lai.

The Change of Régime

When the Japanese suddenly capitulated in August 1945, after the bombing of Hiroshima and Nagasaki, both the Kuomintang and the Communists were taken by surprise. The latter had been waging guerilla warfare against the Japanese in northern China for five years and now prepared to accept the surrender of the enemy garrisons there. But Chiang succeeded in countering their every move and forbade the Communists to enter the larger towns and cities. The stage was set for civil war, stalled off for a time by negotiations between the two parties. An interview between Mao Tse-tung and Chiang K'ai-shek was arranged at Chungking in October 1945. Mao flew down in an American plane, his personal safety being guaranteed by the American government. But the interview came to nothing.

Kuomintang troops re-entered Nanking in March 1946 to receive the official surrender of the Japanese forces there, but they got a cool welcome from the populace. By November 1946 civil war had broken out in earnest. At first the nationalist armies made great headway, occupying town after town in Communist-held territory; in February 1947 they occupied Yenan, the Communist capital since 1934. But thereafter the tide turned and it became clear to everyone that the days of the Kuomintang were numbered.

In August 1947, led by Lin-piao, their outstanding general, the Communist armies won their first signal victory, in Manchuria. By 1948 they controlled all northern China, including Yenan. In October 1948 began the siege of Peking and Tientsin, last nationalist-held cities in northern China; both fell in February 1949. The Communist government was now set up in Peking; at its head was Mao Tse-tung, who 30 years before (in 1917) had been assistant librarian at Peking University.

Chiang was fighting a losing battle. The economic situation of the Kuomintang was desperate. Life was increasingly difficult for peasants, workers, businessmen, small functionaries, students and intellectuals alike, especially in the big cities. Chinese money lost value almost hourly. In Shanghai the crisis reached its peak in December 1948.

The crucial battle of the civil war was fought at Hsuchow, north of Nanking, in March 1949. Twenty Kuomintang divisions were routed. Chiang K'ai-shek resigned from his position as President of the Republic of China.

In April 1949 the Communist armies crossed the Yangtze, entered Nanking and Wuchang, and occupied the entire Yangtze Valley. In May they entered Shanghai. General Chen-yi, former student in France and former factory-worker in the Renault automobile plant outside Paris, was elected mayor of the city.

By September 1949 Chiang K'ai-shek, his government and the remnants of his armies had evacuated continental China and taken refuge at Formosa.

In October 1949, at Peking, Mao Tse-tung proclaimed the Chinese People's Republic.

MONGOLIA

MANCHURIA

Yellow River

Peking

Tientsin

SINKIANG

SHANSI

SHANTUNG

SHENSI

Grand Canal

Wei-Ho

TIBET

Nanking

SZECHWAN

Shanghai

Wuchang

Hangchow

Yangtze

Chungking

KIANGSI

FORMOSA

Si-kiang

Canton

Macao

Hong-kong

HAINAN

This volume, prepared by Robert Delpire in collaboration with Henri Cartier-Bresson, was printed by Maîtres-Imprimeurs Draeger at Montrouge. Finished the thirtieth day of June, nineteen hundred and fifty-six. Binding by Engel at Malakoff.

The captions of the photographs were written by Henri Cartier-Bresson.

Several photographs first appeared in Life Magazine, for which they were taken, and then in various illustrated magazines. For these Henri Cartier-Bresson received the prize for the best photographic reporting job of the year 1947 awarded by the Overseas Press Club.

Photographs nº. 56 and nº. 121, which first appeared in "Images à la sauvette", have been reprinted here with the kind permission of Editions Verve.

Published in the same series :
From Incas to Indios. Photographs by Werner Bischof, Robert Frank and Pierre Verger. Text by Manuel Tunon de Lara.

Fiesta in Pamplona. Photographs by Inge Morath. Text by Dominique Aubier.